Cross Country Routes of the SOUTHERN Railway

by Terry Gough

Oxford Publishing Company

ISBN 0-86093-267-2

Typesetting by:
Aquarius Typesetting Services,
New Milton, Hants.

Printed in Great Britain by
Netherwood Dalton & Co. Ltd.,
Huddersfield, Yorks.

ABBREVIATIONS USED THROUGHOUT THIS VOLUME

The notes relating to patterns of services and other activities refer to the period covered by the photographs unless otherwise stated and are, of necessity, only generalizations. I have, as previously, used the twelve hour clock and the station names in use at the time of photographing.

BR . . . . British Railways
GWR . . . . Great Western Railway
LBSCR . . . . . . .London, Brighton & South Coast Railway
LCDR . . . . .London, Chatham & Dover Railway
LMSR . . . . .London, Midland & Scottish Railway
LNER . . . . London & North Eastern Railway
LSWR . . . . .London & South Western Railway
MSWJR . . . . Midland & South Western Junction Railway
SDJR . . . . Somerset & Dorset Joint Railway
SECR . . . . South Eastern & Chatham Railway
SER . . . . South Eastern Railway
SR . . . . .Southern Railway

BC . . . . .brake composite
BCL . . . . .brake composite lavatory
BT . . . . brake third
BTK . . . . brake third corridor
C . . . . .composite
CK . . . . composite corridor
FK . . . . first corridor
T . . . . third
TK . . . . third corridor
TO . . . . .third open

The SECR line between Redhill and Guildford saw a considerable variety of motive power right up to dieselization. Class S15, No. 30835 enters Betchworth with the 8.20a.m. Reading South to Redhill on 28th April 1962.

Title page:
Victoria was the starting point for steam operated services to Sussex. Class N, No. 31410 makes an impressive sight filling the roof space with steam on the morning of 13th February 1962.

Published by:
Oxford Publishing Company,
Link House,
West Street,
POOLE, Dorset.

Contents

Introduction

Many books have been written about branch lines. As a result, most are well documented both in terms of their historical development and photographically. The main line too has received wide coverage, but not so the secondary lines or cross-country routes. This is particularly true of the Southern Railway, where they existed in a no man's land, being neither part of the suburban system, nor attracting the glamour of the main lines radiating from the Southern's London termini.

This book is a pictorial record of the secondary routes of the former Southern Railway, from the late 1950s until their modernization or closure. Some are alternative routes between two towns served by a main line. In Kent, Ashford could be reached from London either via Tonbridge, (the main line) or, at a more leisurely pace, via Maidstone. In Sussex, there were numerous ex-LBSCR lines connecting London with the south coast resorts. Others were cross-country lines of considerable length, such as the ex-SECR line from Tonbridge to Redhill and Reading. I have given substantial coverage of this line in view of its significant trespass into LSWR territory. The LSWR itself had relatively few secondary routes and most of these, which were

in Hampshire, were dieselized from the late 1950s. There were none at all in East Devon, although many places were served by branch lines. West of Exeter, the LSWR fanned out to Plymouth, Padstow, Bude and Ilfracombe. All these destinations had through trains from Waterloo and routes to the first and last named places in particular could be regarded as main lines. The North Cornwall line to Padstow had more the air of a cross-country service and I have therefore included this. Whatever the status of the lines beyond Exeter in the period covered by the photographs, the fact remains that their importance had decreased somewhat after nationalization and then dramatically after they were transferred to the Western Region. Today, all that remains for passenger trains is the line towards Ilfracombe, now terminating at Barnstaple Junction, and the section from Plymouth to Bere Alston and Gunnislake.

It is hoped that this book will serve as a reminder of a pleasant, if somewhat slower, mode of travel.

Terry Gough
Woking
1983

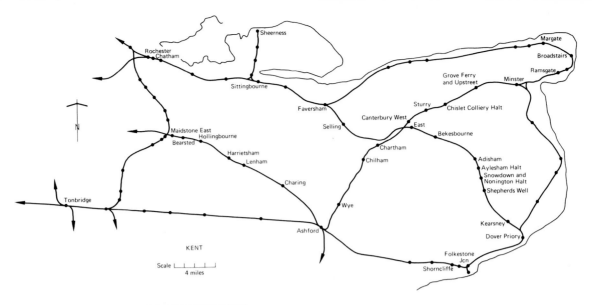

FAVERSHAM TO DOVER PRIORY DIRECT

The north Kent towns of Rochester, Chatham, Sittingbourne and Faversham were served by main line trains from Victoria to Margate and Ramsgate. Dover was normally reached from Charing Cross via the SER main line through Tonbridge, but there was also a secondary route to Dover leaving the North Kent line at Faversham, this being the LCDR route. Most trains started at Faversham, although there were occasional through trains from Sheerness-on-Sea. London to Ramsgate trains often included a portion for this route and this portion was dropped either at Gillingham or Faversham.

Plate 1: The standard 5MT 4-6-0s were built from 1951 onwards. No. 73086, not long outshopped, steams through Chatham on 7th October 1956. These engines were found all over the BR network and about 30 were allocated to the Southern Region. The train is the 10.35 a.m. from Victoria to Ramsgate, with through coaches for Dover Priory.

Plate 2: On 12th March 1959, Class L1, No. 31789 is seen attaching the 11.21 a.m. from Dover Priory on to the rear of the 11.15 a.m. Ramsgate to Victoria at Faversham. The L1s were built in 1926 by the Southern Railway and were the last of the line of a development from SECR 4-4-0 express engines. Some of the class survived the Kent electrification, which made so many steam locomotives redundant, and were transferred to the Western Section of the Region.

Plate 3: The combined train leaves Faversham for Victoria behind 'Battle of Britain' class, No. 34085 *501 Squadron*. Note the third rail in position and recently extended platform in preparation for electrification.

Plate 4: Sandwiched between two coaches at Sittingbourne, en route for Dover on 12th March 1959, is Class H, No. 31512. This most unusual train was one of two used for crew training purposes in the months preceding the introduction of electric multiple units throughout Kent. The coaches were from ex-LBSCR push-pull sets Nos. 504 and 651. In the station is a Class H tank locomotive on a train from Sheerness-on-Sea. A Class C locomotive is shunting in the yard.

Plate 5: Class 4MT, No. 42095 is photographed near Snowdown & Nonington Halt with the 3.43 p.m Canterbury East to Dover Priory with Bulleid set No. 964 on 26th March 1959. A substantial number of LMS-designed 2-6-4 tanks were allocated to the Southern Region. The halt served the nearby colliery and mining community. For some years an SECR Class P, 0-6-0 tank engine was used here on colliery shunting duties.

Plate 6: Class 4MT, No. 42077 is seen with the 4.18 p.m. Dover Priory to Faversham near Aylesham Halt on 26th March 1959. On this section of the line there were three stations in two miles, Aylesham being the middle one.

Plate 7: Class N15, No. 30799 *Sir Ironside*, over an hour late, with the 4.05 p.m. Faversham to Dover Priory, pounding along near Aylesham Halt, on 26th March 1959. The 'King Arthur' class (N15s) were designed by Urie as the last LSWR express engines. Twenty were built between 1918 and 1923. With minor modifications further batches were built by the SR. Some, specifically for the Eastern Section, were built by the North British Locomotive Company and others, allocated mainly to the Central Section, had six wheeled tenders.

THE EAST KENT COAST

Local trains served the stations on the East Kent Coast. Some services were remnants of trains from London and others ran only between Margate and Dover or Folkestone. Margate and Ramsgate were also starting points for some trains to Reading, and particularly in the summer months, for the through trains to other Regions. Because of early competition between the SER and LCDR, railways in this part of Kent were unnecessarily complex. Both Margate and Ramsgate had three stations. In 1926 new lines were constructed in the Ramsgate area which greatly simplified services. As part of the same development, both towns were provided with new stations.

Plate 8 (below):   One of the last steam worked Kent services was the 7.24 a.m. from London Bridge, which took 3½ hours to reach Margate via Ashford and Dover. Class D1, No. 31739 is pictured near London Bridge on 5th June 1961, a few days before electrification of the Kent lines.

Plate 9 (top right):   Class C locomotives, Nos. 31150 and 31004 haul empty carriage stock, consisting of set No. 460 from Margate, at Folkestone Junction on 26th March 1959. An up boat train with 'Battle of Britain' class, No. 34067 *Tangmere* is waiting to leave, on the right, for Victoria. On the left is Class R1, No. 31107, in store after being deposed from the Folkestone Harbour branch by GWR pannier tanks.

Plate 10 (bottom right):   On the same day, Class 4MT, No. 42076 is seen with the 12.25 p.m. Shorncliffe to Minster (all stations), leaving Folkestone Junction. The stock is a Maunsell brake third and three standard coaches in original BR livery. The engine shed can be seen behind the last two coaches.

Plate 11: The most powerful and famous British 4-4-0s were the 'Schools' class, introduced in 1930 and used extensively on Kent main line services. No. 30939 *Leatherhead,* with the 2.41 p.m. Margate to London, leaves Ramsgate with set No. 972 on 25th August 1960. Despite the impressive motive power, this train ran all stations to Ashford and then Tonbridge. Instead of continuing to London on the main line it ran fast to Redhill, using the ex-LBSCR Brighton line to East Croydon, and eventually back on to the SECR to terminate at Cannon Street over four hours later. This is, in fact, the original SER route to London *(see Plate 28).*

Plate 12: The same service at Margate with another 'Schools' class locomotive, No. 30924 *Haileybury* over a year earlier on 12th March 1959. The water crane in the foreground is of standard Southern Railway design.

ASHFORD TO RAMSGATE DIRECT

A direct service ran between Ashford and Ramsgate, the ex-SER route, passing through Canterbury West. Even today, Canterbury still has two stations, the other being Canterbury East on the ex-LCDR Faversham to Dover line *(Plates 5–7)*. From Canterbury West, there were also lines to Whitstable and to Folkestone via the Elham Valley. These were closed in 1931 and 1940 respectively. There was a connection between the East and West stations which had been long since disused when flooding suddenly struck the North Kent coast on the last day of January 1953, washing away a substantial length of main line in the Herne Bay area. The connecting spur was rapidly rehabilitated, to enable London to Margate trains to reach their destination.

Plate 13: A local train from Ramsgate, headed by rebuilt 'West Country' class, No. 34021 *Dartmoor* is seen near Margate on 12th March 1959. Although many services terminated at Margate the nearest engine shed was at Ramsgate, resulting in some unusual workings such as tender first operation and double-heading.

Plate 14: There was one through train from London, via Tonbridge, on weekday evenings, with through coaches which were detached at Ashford. On 21st April 1960, Class C, No. 31218 detaches these coaches, which will form the 6.12 p.m. to Dover via the Canterbury West line, a distance of 43 miles. Dover, by the direct route taken by the front half of the same train, was a mere 17 miles.

Plate 15: Class N, No. 31848 leaves Ashford with the 4.12 p.m. Tonbridge to Margate via Canterbury West on 21st April 1960. The stock consists of Bulleid set No. 91. Smoke deflectors were fitted to all Class N locomotives from 1934. However, No. 31848 ran without deflectors for over a year, following the fitting of new cylinders with outside steam pipes in 1955.

Plate 18 (above): The Ashford break-down train at Minster on 22nd August 1960, hauled by Class K, No. 32340. This class very rarely operated outside the Central Section of the Southern Region, the whole class being allocated to Brighton and Three Bridges sheds. The coach is an ex-SECR birdcage brake third.

Plate 19: There were substantial coal fields in Kent which were well served by rail, both passenger and freight. This is the afternoon miners' train from Chislet Colliery Halt, near Broadstairs on 12th March 1959. The train consists of four SECR ten compartment thirds and an SECR continental brake third, hauled by Class 4MT, No. 42095.

Plate 16 (left upper): Class 4MT, No. 80040 is pictured at Sturry with the 11.44 a.m. Margate to Ashford on 22nd August 1960. Many SER stations had staggered platforms. Instead of the up and down platforms being opposite, they were end on. At Sturry, there was even a level crossing between the platforms.

Plate 17 (left lower): Class 2MT, No. 84021 with the 12.28 p.m. Maidstone East to Margate at Grove Ferry & Upstreet on the same day. There really was a ferry here; a small chain operated system for pedestrians and cars.

Plate 20: BR standard tanks Nos. 82029 and 84029, double-heading Bulleid set No. 94 with the 12.28 p.m. Maidstone East to Margate via Canterbury West, approaches its destination on 12th March 1959.

MAIDSTONE TO ASHFORD

From Victoria to Maidstone East, an electric service was provided from July 1939, and although the line continued east to Ashford, this section was not electrified until 1962. In the intervening years, a steam operated service ran between Maidstone and Ashford. There were usually good connections with the Victoria service in both the up and down directions at Maidstone. Boat trains for the Kentish ports usually ran via Tonbridge, but occasionally they would take the Maidstone line, for example, due to engineering works on the main line.

Plate 21 (right upper):   A boat train at Victoria routed via Maidstone East and hauled by 'Battle of Britain' class, No. 34077 ▷
603 Squadron on 28th May 1961. Many of the 'Battle of Britain' and 'West Country' class locomotives were rebuilt by BR, resulting in a more conventional, but still attractive, outline.

Plate 22 (right lower):   Pulling away from Bearsted on 28th March 1961 is Class 4MT, No. 80085 with the 4.31 p.m. ▷
Ashford to Maidstone East, with set No. 955.

Plate 23: The same formation seen on the return working from Maidstone, which ran through to Margate. The engine is in a rather grimy condition, emphasized by the filthy black smoke being emitted.

Plate 24: Class 4MT, No. 80034 passes Hollingbourne box with the 2.02 p.m. Ramsgate to Maidstone East on 28th March 1961. Both engine and coaches are considerably cleaner than those in *Plate 23*. Note the S E C R fluted gas lamp on the right.

Plate 25: A down freight passes Lenham, hauled by Class Q1, No. 33033 on 28th March 1961. There was a substantial amount of freight generated at Lenham, where there were also carriage sidings to relieve pressure in the Ashford area. The Class Q1 locomotive was built to a wartime design by Bulleid for heavy freight work and although inelegant, was both a powerful and reliable machine.

Plate 26: Class Q1s were not commonly seen on passenger trains. No. 33038 stands at Ashford with the 4.35 p.m. from Maidstone East on 21st April 1960. There were forty of these engines, one of which has been preserved.

TONBRIDGE TO REDHILL

The line from Tonbridge to Redhill formed part of the SER main line from London to Dover prior to the building of the direct route to Tonbridge through Sevenoaks in 1868. The line declined in importance as a result and became more of a local service for towns and villages between Tonbridge and Redhill. The line also formed the first section of a cross-country line to Guildford and Reading although it was not regarded as a properly integrated system until the end of 1965. It was used by a substantial amount of freight traffic between the Kent coast and the Midlands as it offered a bypass around London. The line has always been of considerable strategic significance because of this connection to the Midlands and because it served the Aldershot area. Passenger trains from other regions to the Kentish holiday resorts also used this line. All trains needed to reverse at Redhill, where the route intersected the London to Brighton main line. The line still exists today in its entirety and is now of potential value in relation to the proposed Channel Tunnel development.

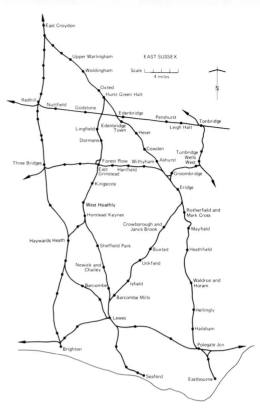

Plate 27: Class N, No. 31826 and set No. 186 stop at Leigh Halt with the 9.16 a.m. Redhill to Tonbridge train. 'Leigh' was the original spelling of the name and was changed to 'Lyghe' in 1917. By the time this photograph was taken, on 19th May 1961, it had just reverted to the original spelling.

Plate 28: Class V, No. 30938 *St Olave's,* with the 2.41 p.m. Margate to Cannon Street, crosses over the ex-LBSCR Oxted to Tunbridge Wells line at Edenbridge on 4th April 1960 *(see also Plates 11 & 12).* Only four of the nine vehicles are passenger coaches, the remainder being vans. Although there was no rail connection with the Oxted line here, there was a spur a little further on at Crowhurst Junction to connect with the Oxted to East Grinstead line. This connection has now been lifted.

Plate 29: Class 4MT, No. 80143 pictured at Godstone with the 11.01 a.m. Tonbridge to Redhill train on 8th September 1962. The village of Godstone was three miles away, but the presence of the railway gave rise to a small development known as South Godstone.

Plate 30: Class 4MT, No. 80018 leaves Nutfield with the 10.35 a.m. Tonbridge to Redhill on 8th September 1962. The signal box is of a rather uncommon design and blends well with the local architecture. From Nutfield, the railway forms an almost continuous straight line to Ashford, 46 miles away.

REDHILL TO GUILDFORD

The short stretch from Redhill to Reigate was electrified in 1939 and had a frequent shuttle service. The steam service continued beyond Reigate along the edge of the Surrey Hills, through Dorking, to join the Waterloo to Portsmouth main line at Shalford Junction, just south of Guildford. Here again it interacted with the pre-war electrified lines. Even today this section is not electrified but is mainly operated by diesel units.

Plate 31: Class S15, No. 30835 leaves Betchworth with the 8.20 a.m. Reading South to Redhill on 28th April 1962. The station was originally called Betchworth & Boxhill, but the name Boxhill is now used by the station nearer the foot of the hill on the ex-LBSCR Leatherhead to Horsham line. The buildings on the right of the train belonged to a quarry and lime-works which had a small steam operated railway, including transfer sidings to British Railways. Apart from the standard gauge, there were two differing narrow gauges within the quarry. One of the narrow gauge engines is now preserved at the nearby Brockham Narrow Gauge Museum.

Plate 32: Most passenger trains were worked by Moguls. Class U, No. 31638 leaves Dorking Town, on 28th April 1962, for Redhill with the 9.03 a.m. from Reading South. Between nationalization and the arrival of the Moguls, there was a fascinating variety of motive power, with classes representative of all three SR pre-grouping companies in evidence. Dorking was also served by the line from Leatherhead to Horsham, which passed a little east of the town. The two lines were connected, as a wartime measure, but the spur was removed in 1947.

Plate 34 (below): By Southern Region standards, the Redhill to Reading line had an intensive freight service. Class N, No. 31842, on a Redhill bound freight, passes through Gomshall & Shere on 28th April 1962.

Plate 33 (left upper): On 28th April 1962, Class N, No. 31820 is seen at Gomshall & Shere with the 9.45 a.m. Reading South to Redhill. The GWR van seen on the train is an unusual sight on the Southern Region in contrast to Southern vans used on the Western Region. There were extensive sandpits here with a rail connection but the site is now occupied by a caravan distributor.

Plate 35: Locomotives from other regions were occasional visitors on through trains. GWR 'Manor' class, No. 7808 *Cookham Manor*, deputizing for a Southern locomotive on a local train, with set No. 974, makes its way through Shere Cutting on 27th July 1963. The line was steeply graded most of the way from Redhill, which, with heavy summer trains, caused some problems on wet days.

Plate 36: An unidentified Class U locomotive leaves Chilworth & Albury with the 12.34 p.m. Redhill to Reading train. In the background is the small yard with wagons for the local coal merchant. To the right is the public house, a feature of many country stations.

Plate 39 (right upper): A short section of the ex-LSWR London to Portsmouth main line, near Guildford, was used by Reading to Redhill trains. Class N, No. 31411 nears Shalford Junction with the 9.03 a.m. from Reading South on 6th April 1963.

Plate 37: Class U, No. 31638 is seen at Chilworth & Albury with a train for Guildford later in the day. The small waiting shelter was typical of those found throughout the SECR system and indeed on many stations rebuilt by the SR.

Plate 38: Class U, No. 31639 hauls the 9.45 a.m. from Reading South, and is seen at Shalford on 15th May 1964. It is noticeable that both the brake thirds are in the middle of the train, a result of splitting the four coach Maunsell sets used on this line into two coach sets. There was a small engine shed at Shalford, long since closed, which was a sub-shed of Redhill. There was little point in retaining this after the grouping, when there was a main shed just round the corner at Guildford.

Plate 40 (below): Guildford was a station of variety, with trains from all three SR pre-grouping companies and occasional inter-regional trains. The motive power depot, sandwiched between the station and the tunnel, had an allocation of antiquities including Classes 0395, 700 and B4. It had also been the home of *Ironside* and the last remaining Class L12 and S11 locomotives. Class N, No. 31412 prepares to leave for Redhill with the 8.20a.m. from Reading, on 6th April 1963.

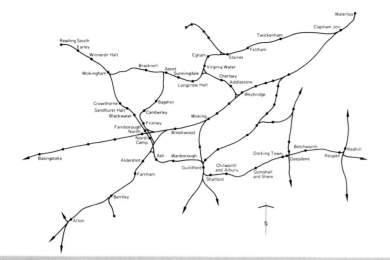

SOUTH WEST LONDON

Scale |___|___|___|___|
4 miles

From Guildford, SECR trains had running powers over the LSWR to Ash Junction, from whence they ran on their own line through to Reading South. There was a motive power depot at Reading South, but this, and the station itself, was closed in 1965. The site is now a car-park. The present service from Guildford terminates in a bay at Reading's Western Region main line station, formerly called Reading General. This bay is shared with the Southern Region service to Waterloo, via Staines, and is rather less than adequate for the job than was the separate Southern terminus.

Plate 41 (above):   On 27th August 1960, ex-GWR Class 4300 Mogul, No. 5385, approaches the junction with the ex-LSWR main line, which is situated just north of Guildford Station. It is hauling Bulleid set No. 85 and forms the 8.20a.m. from Reading South.

Plate 42 (right upper):   On the first day of 1965, Class Q1, No. 33018 passes Wood Street with the Guildford breakdown ▷ crane. Wood Street is situated between Guildford and Wanborough. The rolling stock consists of converted LSWR 'Ironclad' coaches, some of which are still used today by the engineer's department.

Plate 43 (right centre):   Tank engine workings were unusual on the Guildford to Reading line. Class 4MT, No. 80151 with ▷ two coach Maunsell set No. 456 and four Bulleid coaches, crosses the Basingstoke Canal near Aldershot Junction on 1st January 1965. The canal has joined the ranks of many railways in that it is the subject of a restoration scheme.

Plate 44 (right lower):   There was an electric service from Guildford to Aldershot which, with the Reading to Redhill ▷ steam service, provided three passenger trains per hour between Guildford and Ash in each direction. Freight trains had to fit in between these services and Class U, No. 31791 is seen on a Guildford bound freight near Wanborough on 1st January 1965. The electric service still operates, as does the Reading line with Western Region diesel multiple units. There is, additionally, a semi-fast service from Reading to Gatwick Airport.

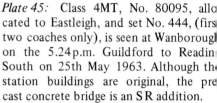

Plate 47 (right upper): On 5th Ma
1963, all trains from Reading Sou
were terminated at Ash due to enginee
ing works towards Guildford. As
common on such events, special bus
were provided to enable passenge
to complete the journey to Guildfor
Class N, No. 31868 is seen at Ash wit
Bulleid set No. 977 after working th
1.50 p.m. from Reading.

Plate 45: Class 4MT, No. 80095, allo
cated to Eastleigh, and set No. 444, (firs
two coaches only), is seen at Wanboroug
on the 5.24 p.m. Guildford to Readin
South on 25th May 1963. Although th
station buildings are original, the pre
cast concrete bridge is an S R addition.

Plate 46: Class Q1, No. 33035 leave
Ash, in atrocious weather, on 14th Marc
1964, with a special tour of local lines
The stock is push-pull set No. 610 and
loose Maunsell open third. There was
small engine shed at Ash and althoug
this was closed shortly before nationali
zation, the building still stands and i
privately owned by a local company.

Plate 48 (right lower): The return work
ing, tender first operated right throug
to Reading. Tender first working wa
fairly unusual on the Southern, even o
freight trains. The bay platform, fron
which a shuttle service to Aldershot usec
to run, is on the right where the engine
shed was also situated.

Plate 49: Class U, No. 31625 awaits departure from North Camp with the 8.45 a.m. Redhill to Reading South on 30th May 1963. Ash and North Camp were the nearest SECR stations to Aldershot, which was on the LSWR. The railways, quite correctly, anticipated that the army would generate considerable business for them. This may have been the reason for naming North Camp originally as North Camp, Aldershot.

Plate 50: Class U, No. 31631 pauses at North Camp with the 9.45 a.m. Reading South to Redhill on 30th May 1963. Over the years, the name of this station changed five times, all names, except the present one, including reference to Aldershot.

Plate 51: Class 4MT, No. 80138 passes beneath the ex-LSWR Waterloo to Bournemouth main line just east of Farnborough. The train is the 1.50 p.m. Reading South to Redhill on 26th March 1964. The leading vehicle is of LNER origin. There was a connecting spur between the two lines, but it was rarely used and has now been taken up.

Plate 52: Class N, No. 31869 and Bulleid set No. 92 pulls away from Farnborough North with the 4.20 p.m. Reading South to Redhill on 26th March 1964. Farnborough was also served by the LSWR, whose station on the main line, was only a few minutes walk away. Both stations are still open.

Plate 53: Standard Class 4MT, No. 76031, with BR stock, is pictured near Farnborough North earlier the same day, with the 3.35 p.m. from Reading South. Modern stock was uncommon on this line where Maunsell coaches were used almost right up to dieselization.

Plate 54: Hardly a taxing load for Class N, No. 31831, as it leaves Farnborough North on 26th March 1964 with two coach set No. 460. The train is the 2.50 p.m. Reading South to Redhill.

Plate 55: In dismal weather on 25th May 1963, Class Q1, No. 33035, deputizing for a failed Mogul, is seen near Crowthorne with the 12.35 p.m. from Reading South. Still in army territory, the main purpose of Crowthorne was to serve the nearby college of Wellington. Until 1928, the station was named after the college.

VICTORIA TO OXTED

Despite the extensive electrification of the suburban system, it was still possible in the 1960s to travel steam hauled from Victoria to Clapham Junction and East Croydon and thence call at all stations to Oxted. In the early days, ownership was rather complicated, being LBSCR from Victoria to Croydon, then LBSCR/SER joint. This was the London end of an extensive system of steam operated lines which fanned out to Tunbridge Wells, Eastbourne, Lewes and Brighton. All that is left today is the truncated Victoria to Lewes line which terminates at Uckfield and the Oxted to East Grinstead line, both of which are diesel multiple unit operated *(see map at Plate 27).*

Plate 56: Class 4MT, No. 80142 stands at Victoria with the 10.08 a.m. to Tunbridge Wells West via East Grinstead on 13th February 1962.

Plate 57: A welcome change from the endless succession of electric units. Class 4MT, No. 80040 with the 2.09 p.m. Victoria to Tunbridge Wells West is seen at Clapham Junction. First class accommodation was provided on these trains and it was thus possible to travel from Clapham Junction and Victoria, first class, although the tickets were still 'Southern Railway', even in August 1962.

Plate 58: Motive power, in the form of Class 4MT, No. 75069, was provided by Stewarts Lane on 28th May 1961 for the 9.38 a.m. Victoria to Brighton. This train, which is seen at Wandsworth Common, ran via Oxted and Eridge and took twice the time to reach Brighton by this route compared with the main line.

Plate 59: From South Croydon to Crowhurst Junction *(see Plate 28)*, just beyond Oxted, the line was operated jointly. SER trains, thereafter, proceeded to Tonbridge and LBSCR trains continued southward to East Grinstead. Class U1, No. 31898 heads the 1.55 p.m. Brighton to Victoria train near Woldingham with set No. 188.

Plate 60: On 5th September 1959, Class U1, No. 31899 with the 3.38 p.m. from Victoria storms up the 1 in 100 bank near Woldingham and darkens the sky in the process. This train divided at Eridge for Brighton and Eastbourne.

OXTED TO TUNBRIDGE WELLS DIRECT

At Hurst Green Junction, just south of Oxted, the line from Victoria divided. One line continued south to East Grinstead, (the joint line as far as Crowhurst Junction), and the other turned south east to Ashurst Junction. The latter was LBSCR all the way from Hurst Green. In BR days, many of the through trains from London ran to East Grinstead, either terminating there or continuing on to Tunbridge Wells. The direct line between Oxted and Ashurst Junction was usually operated by push-pull units connecting with the London services at Oxted. The push-pull trains also ran on to Tunbridge Wells. However, some trains from London would take the direct route through Ashurst and then run to Tunbridge Wells, Eastbourne or Brighton.

Plate 61 (right upper): Hurst Green Halt was situated just north of the junction of the same name. The summer after this photograph was taken, a new station was opened to serve Hurst Green, and the old halt was closed. Class H, No. 31521, with push-pull set No. 660 is pictured at the junction with the 2.00 p.m. Tunbridge Wells West to Oxted train on 14th April 1960.

Plate 62 (right lower): It always seemed incongruous to see push-pull trains composed of pre-grouping motive power and stock interspersed with Bulleid Pacifics and BR standard express engines on this line. 'West Country' class, No. 34009 *Lyme Regis* heads the 1.55 p.m. Brighton to Victoria, near Hurst Green, on 14th April 1960.

Plate 65 (right upper): On 23rd March 1961, a solitary passenger at Cowden reflected the situation on so many secondary and branch lines at that time. The train is the 11.04a.m. Oxted to Tunbridge Wells West with Class H, No 31278 hauling set No. 652.

Plate 66 (right lower): Class H, No. 31162 pulls away from Cowden with the 1.00p.m. Tunbridge Wells West to Oxted on 23rd March 1961. The lattice post starter is of LSWR design and replaced the original LBSCR signal after the grouping.

Plate 63: Class E4, No. 32581, with push-pull set No. 652, stands at Edenbridge Town with the 7.24p.m. Oxted to Tunbridge Wells West on the evening of 14th April 1960. This train is not being worked in the push-pull mode as E4s were not so fitted. The significance of the chalked 'L' and 'R' is not clear, except that it presumably meant 'left' and 'right'. There was also a large 'L' on the smokebox door.

Plate 64: A pleasant day in April 1960 saw Class 4MT, No. 75075 with the 3.50p.m. Victoria to Eastbourne and Brighton, near Edenbridge Town. In pre-grouping days, through coaches for Tunbridge Wells were slipped at Edenbridge.

Plate 67 (left upper): Ashurst, a quiet country station, with the local train, apparently, with all the time in the world. Class H, No. 31543, and set No. 652 form the 1.04 p.m. Oxted to Tunbridge Wells West on 2nd September 1961. Behind the platform fence is an ex-LSWR covered van.

Plate 68 (left lower): In contrast to the hourly push-pull train, was the evening seven coach train from London, which divided at Ashurst. Class U1, No. 31892 is seen with the 4.48 p.m. from Victoria on 23rd March 1961. Class Q, No. 30537 waits in the yard until the front portion of the train leaves for Brighton.

Plate 69: The rear three coaches of the 4.48 p.m. from London prepare to leave Ashurst for Tunbridge Wells West behind No. 30537 as twilight approaches.

Plate 70: The line right through from Oxted passed through pleasant countryside, typified by this photograph taken near Ashurst on an afternoon in September 1961. Class H, No. 31544 propels set No. 656 and forms the 4.38 p.m. Tonbridge to Oxted train.

◁ *Plate 71 (left upper):* On 2nd September 1961, Class H, No. 31543 and set No. 652 approach Ashurst Junction, where the two lines from Oxted recombine, with the 4.04 p.m. from Oxted. The signal indicates that the train is bound for Tunbridge Wells rather than Eridge as this is also the junction for these two destinations.

◁ *Plate 72 (left lower):* Class H, No. 31162, with the 2.39 p.m. to Oxted, prepares to leave Tunbridge Wells West on 23rd March 1961. In the background is a Class 4MT on the Eastbourne service. The motive power depot is behind the push-pull train. This shed was responsible for providing the Class H tanks for the push-pull services in the area and the 2-6-4 tanks for the London and Eastbourne services. Larger engines for the London trains were provided by Stewarts Lane and Brighton.

OXTED TO TUNBRIDGE WELLS VIA EAST GRINSTEAD

East Grinstead had two stations, known as High and Low Level. They were both directly accessible from London, the line from Oxted diverging at St. Margarets Junction about a mile from East Grinstead. There was also a connection between the high and low levels, used for transferring empty stock and turning engines. This connecting line ran past the site of the original terminus of the line from Three Bridges. Once the High Level Station was built, Three Bridges trains used this station until the line was closed in 1967. After closure of the service from Lewes, (the Bluebell Line), all trains used the High Level Station but the present day service has reverted to using the Low Level Station.

Plate 73: Class 4MT, No. 80142 is seen with the 5.25 p.m. to Victoria early in June 1960. The tail end of the Victoria to Tunbridge Wells West train is on the far left, the push-pull service from Three Bridges is in the centre and the train to Three Bridges is ready to depart on the far right.

Plate 74: Class 4MT, No. 80095 enter Hartfield with the 5.47p.m. Tunbridg Wells West to Victoria, with set No. 19 at the front of the train. The section between Ashurst Junction and Eas Grinstead was single track.

Plate 76 (right upper): Class 4MT, No 80012, hauls the 2.08p.m. Victoria t Tunbridge Wells West, via East Grinstead on 23rd March 1961. The train i approaching Groombridge Junctio where the London and Eridge line diverge. This junction forms the secon apex of a triangle, the other junction being at Ashurst, *(see Plate 71)*, an Birchden.

Plate 77 (right lower): Class 4MT, No 80082 is pictured with the 3.47p.m. from Tunbridge Wells West, at Groombridge o 23rd March 1961. This train, which ra via East Grinstead, terminated at Eas Croydon. For some extraordinary reason it then ran empty to London Bridge to form one of the down rush hour trains.

Plate 75: Class 4MT, No. 42106 is pic tured at Withyham with the 10.08a.m Victoria to Tunbridge Wells West on 2n May 1958. Although built to a design by Stanier and numbered in the Midlan Region series, these engines were not fa from home as they were built at Brighto in 1950.

Plate 78: Departure from Tunbridge Wells West on 23rd March 1961 with Class 4MT, No. 80144 heading the 2.47 p.m. to Victoria. The first two coaches are ten compartment all thirds, not particularly comfortable for a long journey.

TUNBRIDGE WELLS TO EASTBOURNE

This line was built from south to north and became known, very early on in its life, as the 'Cuckoo Line'. In 1849, a service was opened from Eastbourne as far as Hailsham and the line did not reach Tunbridge Wells (West) until 1880. The single track connection to the SECR at Tunbridge Wells (now Central) was made the following year and although the line was LBSCR throughout, the SECR had running powers to Eastbourne. The line was steeply graded, in several places as much as 1 in 50 and it abounded in sharp curves with severe speed restrictions. A fixed interval service was not introduced until the summer of 1956 as part of a scheme covering all services operating on the Tunbridge Wells, Oxted and East Grinstead lines. From this time the motive power was almost exclusively in the hands of the Brighton-built BR standard 2-6-4 tank engines.

Plate 79 (right upper): Class C, No. 31592 prepares to leave Tunbridge Wells West with a pickup freight for Eastbourne. The ▷ shed yard, containing two BR standard Class 4s, is in the background.

Plate 80 (right lower): An hourly service ran between Tunbridge Wells West and Eastbourne. Class 4MT, No. 80154, the ▷ last engine to be built at Brighton, is seen at Groombridge Junction with the 3.39 p.m. to Eastbourne on 23rd March 1961.

Plate 81: An unusual occurrence at Rotherfield & Mark Cross. Class 4MT, No. 80054 and set No. 953 form the 12.45 p.m. from Eastbourne and picks up a horse-box from the bay for Chipping Sodbury on the Western Region. This activity, which took place on 29th March 1961 resulted in the train leaving ten minutes late.

Plate 82: It was usually the down trains which were worked bunker first. Class 4MT, No. 80037 stops at Heathfield with the 3.39 p.m. Tunbridge Wells West to Eastbourne, whilst hauling set No. 90, on 10th August 1962.

Plate 83: The same train passes the 3.45 p.m. from Eastbourne with Class 4MT, No. 80013 in command, at Heathfield. The stock on the up train consists of two Maunsell push-pull sets made redundant by the closure of push-pull operated branch lines elsewhere on the Region.

Plate 84: The pick up freight from Tunbridge Wells is seen at Heathfield, on 14th August 1956, with Class C, No. 31588 in charge. On many Southern lines, freight traffic ran at night owing to the difficulty in finding paths between the regular passenger train workings.

Plate 85: A special working approaches Waldron & Horam hauled by preserved locomotives Class M7, No. 30055 and Class T9, No. 120, the latter in LSWR livery. The effect is rather spoilt by the use of Bulleid and BR stock. This station was originally known as Horeham Road for Waldron and subsequent to the photograph, which was taken on 24th June 1962, merely Horam.

Plate 86: Two engines for two coaches. Push-pull set No. 608, hauled by Class N, No. 31401 and Class 4MT, No. 80016, forms the 1.39 p.m. Tunbridge Wells West to Eastbourne at Hailsham on 13th April 1962. Double-heading on the Southern was unusual as few trains were heavy enough to warrant it. It was, however, used as a means of minimising light engine workings and, of course, giving assistance to an engine in trouble.

Plate 87: Additional trains were run, particularly at peak periods, between Hailsham and Eastbourne. Class E4, No. 32470 and set No. 609 leave Hailsham with the 2.07 p.m. to Eastbourne on 13th April 1962. This train was presumably for the benefit of local people wishing to shop in Eastbourne, which was reached in sixteen minutes.

Plate 88: Later the same day, just south of Hailsham, Class 4MT, No. 80149 is seen on a train from Tunbridge Wells with an ex-LMSR parcels brake van and a BR standard set.

Plate 89: As the evening draws near, an unidentified Class 4MT and set No. 182 work the 4.45 p.m. to Tunbridge Wells West. Although the northern part of the line closed on 14th June 1965, the service was retained between Hailsham and Polegate for a further three years.

Plate 90: Unusual motive power and set formation; Class K, No. 32347 with set No. 248, consisting of two Maunsell brakes and a Bulleid third. The train is the peak hour shuttle between Polegate, on the Lewes to Eastbourne line, and Hailsham, a distance of three miles. This turn was often worked by a tender engine provided by Brighton and, on occasions, even a 'West Country' Pacific was used.

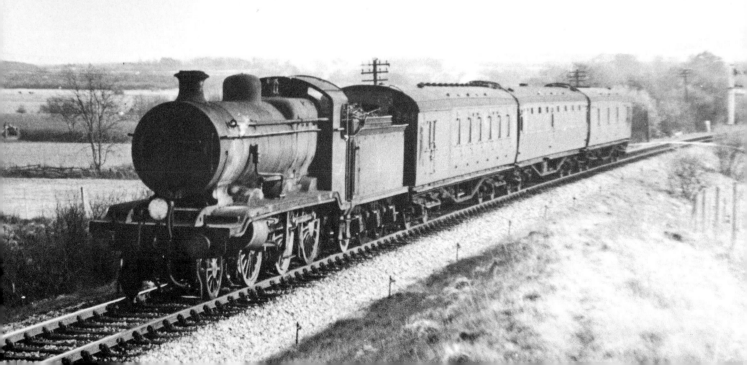

TONBRIDGE TO BRIGHTON

This line was also built from the south reaching Uckfield from Lewes in 1858 and Tunbridge Wells West ten years later. It was heavily graded, at least at the northern end, with the summit just south of Crowborough. The direct connection with the Oxted line between Eridge and Ashurst Junction was not used until 1914. Most trains originated from Tunbridge Wells West until 1956 when an hourly service from Tonbridge was introduced. There was a peak hour service from Victoria via Oxted. Because of restricted clearance in Grove Tunnel, connecting Tunbridge Wells West and the Hastings main line near Tunbridge Wells Central, trains running through to Tonbridge had, of necessity, to be composed exclusively of 'Restriction 1' stock. By 1960, severe shortage of this stock resulted in some Brighton trains starting from Tunbridge Wells West instead of from Tonbridge.

Plate 91: Tunbridge Wells West, complete with large clock tower, was a most impressive station. Class N1, No. 31878 leaves for Tonbridge with the 12.55 p.m. from Brighton, on 23rd March 1961, at the head of set No. 451. The N1 locomotive, of which only six were built, was a three cylinder version of the N class. In the bay platform is the unique push-pull set, No. 659, consisting of an SECR birdcage brake third and a brake composite. It was the latter coach which was the driving vehicle.

Plate 92 (right upper):   On 2nd September 1961, Class N, No. 31869 and set No. 187 form the 2.10 p.m. Tonbridge to Brighton, and is pictured at Groombridge. Some of the stock for the peak hour London services was stored at Groombridge during the day and is just visible beyond the goods shed.

Plate 93 (right lower): 'Battle of Britain' class, No. 34055 *Fighter Pilot* hauls the 1.55 p.m. Brighton to Victoria at Uckfield on 27th March 1961. The road in front of the train is the main A22 from Eastbourne to London and the arrival of trains caused substantial delays to the flow of traffic, particularly on summer weekends. Plans to site the present terminus of the line on the London side of the level crossing have not yet materialized.

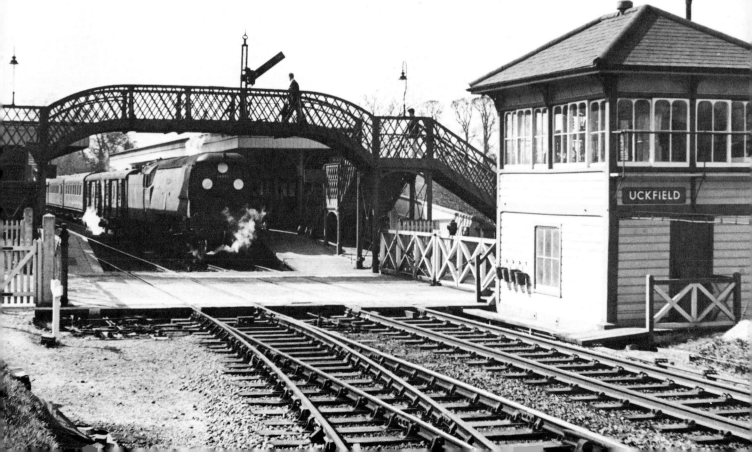

◁ *Plate 94 (left upper):* The pick up freight, with Class K, No. 32339, shunts in Uckfield yard on 27th March 1961. These handsome engines, of which all seventeen still existed at the time of the photograph, were designed in 1913 by Billinton as express freight engines. They were withdrawn en bloc at the end of 1962.

◁ *Plate 95 (left lower):* Emerging from the woods near Uckfield, on 27th March 1961, is Class U1, No. 31904 heading set No. 191 with the 2.10p.m. from Tonbridge. The prototype, No. 31890, was originally built, in 1925, as a Class K1, a three cylinder 2-6-4 tank locomotive. It was rebuilt as a tender engine in 1928. Twenty further engines were newly built as tender engines, at Eastleigh, in 1931.

Plate 96: Barcombe, a typical Sussex village, had two stations, one on the direct East Grinstead to Lewes route and the other, known as Barcombe Mills, on the Eridge to Brighton Line. Class 4MT, No. 80067 leaves the latter station with the 10.38a.m. Victoria to Brighton, hauling set No. 227, on 27th March 1961. Note the fine array of platform oil lamps.

Plate 97: Class N, No. 31861 leaves Barcombe Mills, with the 11.55a.m. Brighton to Tonbridge, at the head of set No. 188, on 27th March 1961. Maunsell Moguls virtually monopolized this line right up to the arrival of the diesels. This, the southern end of the line to Lewes, closed in February 1969.

Plate 98: Lewes, a station with a very cramped layout, had lines radiating to Seaford in the south, Brighton to the west, Eastbourne and Hastings in the east, the main line to Victoria, and the secondary routes to East Grinstead and Eridge. Class N, No. 31865, together with set No. 189, form the 3.10p.m. from Brighton on 8th June 1962. As can be seen in the picture, the line on the left is served by two platforms.

Plate 99 (right upper): Another Mogul, on this occasion, a Class U1, No. 31892, makes up, with set No. 181, the 10.55 a.m. Brighton to Tonbridge train and approaches Lewes on 27th March 1961. This section of the line is still open and is part of the south coast system, electrified in 1935.

Plate 100 (right lower): Evening at Brighton on 8th June 1962, with Class K, No. 32341 and an SR utility van in the parcels bay. The platforms to the left were used by the steam hauled trains for London and Tonbridge.

EAST GRINSTEAD TO LEWES

The most famous of all the Sussex secondary routes was the direct line from East Grinstead to Lewes, the isolated remains between Horsted Keynes and Sheffield Park being the present day Bluebell Railway. The line was closed in 1955, but the Southern Region was forced to reopen it, by a legal quirk, on 7th August the following year. From 1956, until final closure by BR on 16th March 1958, a two hourly service was run between East Grinstead Low Level and Lewes, calling at all stations except Kingscote and Barcombe. During this period, trains usually consisted of a single coach, hauled by whatever motive power Brighton could muster.

Plate 101: The first day of reopening. Class C2X, No. 32442, waits at East Grinstead Low Level, at the head of ex-LBSCR set No. 504, with the 2.28 p.m. to Lewes. In the background, at the High Level Station, is a Three Bridges bound train. It was the brake third from set No. 504 which was later used for crew training in Kent *(see Plate 4)*.

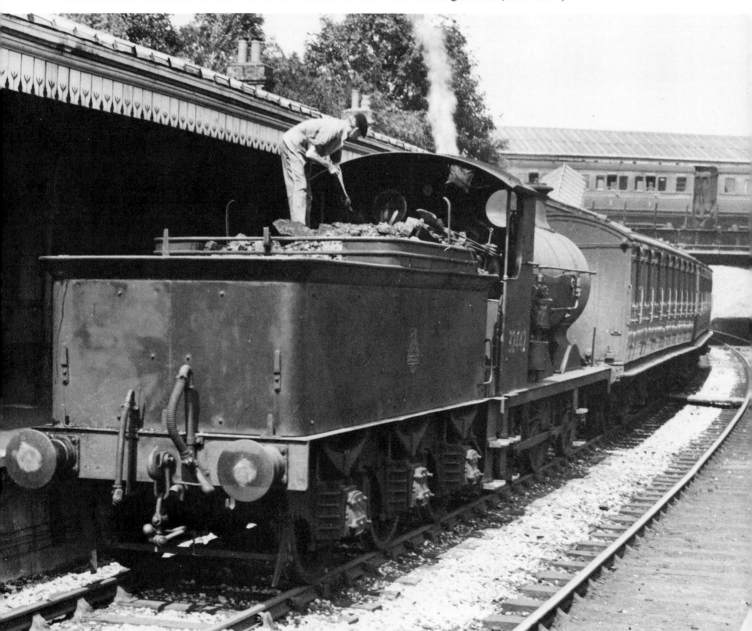

Plate 102 (right upper):   Class E4, No. 32508 heads the 9.30 a.m. Lewes to East Grinstead, with Kingscote in the background. Although the service could be operated with one set, locomotives were changed throughout the day. The coach is ex-LBSCR brake third No. 3847 from push-pull set No. 715. One month later the line was closed, for the second time.

Plate 103 (right lower):   Class 4MT, No. 80150 emerges from West Hoathly Tunnel with the 1.30 p.m. Lewes to East Grinstead train on 18th February 1958. West Hoathly Tunnel was a source of continuous problems, due mainly to excessive water seepage, throughout its existence.

Plate 104: The same formation makes up the 2.28 p.m. from East Grinstead and is seen leaving West Hoathly. The last train on this line was worked by No. 80154 of the same class, but with six coaches.

Plate 105: Class C2X, No. 32442 works the 11.30 a.m. from Lewes and is pictured near Sheffield Park on a bitterly cold February morning in 1958. These engines were rebuilt, over the period 1908 to 1940, from the LBSCR Class C2 locomotives. There was a total of 45 and the majority survived well into nationalization. There were a few withdrawals in the late 1950s, but suddenly, in 1960/61, the vast majority were condemned and by the end of 1961 there were only three left. These three lasted only a few months longer and, regrettably, none of the class now survive.

Plate 106: Ramblers' excursions from London often went to destinations of particular interest to railway enthusiasts. 'Battle of Britain' class, No. 34061 *Kenley* with a train from Victoria, is seen leaving Horsted Keynes on 27th September 1959, after closure to regular traffic and long before the Bluebell Railway reached here. Horsted Keynes was used to store condemned passenger stock, some of which can be seen in the background.

WATERLOO TO READING SOUTH

In addition to the main line services from Waterloo, there was a secondary route, to Reading, which was electrified in 1939. This line saw a regular service of steam hauled local parcels traffic, pick up and inter-regional freight trains. The latter ran either from the Southern Region and joined the Western Region at Reading, or originated on the Midland Region, running via Willesden and thence usually to Feltham. There were branches from the Reading line at Virginia Water and Ascot, both for electric passenger trains and freight trains. It also joined the ex-SECR line, from Guildford, at Wokingham. Although still used by long distance freight trains, its importance has greatly diminished following the closure of Feltham marshalling yards *(see map at Plate 41)*.

Plate 107: A rarity in London, even twenty five years ago. Class T9, No. 30718 is seen on a local freight at Queens Road (Battersea) on 24th September 1958. This was rather a degrading task for a locomotive which had been, at one time, regarded as a most capable express passenger engine. Prior to electrification, T9s were frequently used on the steeply graded LSWR main line to Portsmouth.

Plate 108: The Christmas period always provided additional passenger and mail trains, often using older types of engines and rolling stock. In the suburban electrified area, old 4 SUB electric units were even used to convey parcels in the passenger compartments to the complete exclusion of passengers. A parcels train is seen passing through Twickenham on 27th December 1961, hauled by Class L1, No. 31786.

Plate 109: Most local freight in the London area ran at night due to the intensity of the suburban passenger services. However, there was a regular pick up freight which could be seen at Twickenham mid morning. On 11th August 1965, this was worked by Class S15, No. 30839.

Plate 110: The only steam worked passenger trains were specials. Class Q, No. 30545 together with set No. 770 forms the 'Maunsell Commemorative Railtour' near Longcross Halt on New Year's Day, 1965. It was a pity that the coaches were of Bulleid design. There is no nearby village and the halt, which is on Chobham Common, was opened in 1942 and serves the adjacent military vehicle research establishment.

Plate 111: 'Battle of Britain' class, No. 34086 *219 Squadron* storms up the bank, between Egham and Virginia Water, with westbound freight on a crisp March morning in 1965. Even towards the end of steam, it was unusual to see 'West Country' Pacifics on freight trains other than in the West of England.

Plate 112: There was a daily pick up freight on the Chertsey loop, which joins Virginia Water with Weybridge on the main line from Waterloo. Class Q1, No. 33010 is seen heading for Weybridge and is pictured, near Addlestone, on 31st July 1963. The first vehicle is a standard SR 20T brake van.

Plate 113: A train consisting solely of brake vans, with Class S15, No. 30837 in charge, is seen at Chertsey on 21st August 1963. On the left is the water tower of the former engine shed. The shed was closed on electrification and demolished in the 1960s, only a few days before the author arrived to photograph and measure it.

Plate 114: Class S15, No. 30833 arrives at Weybridge on the pick up freight from Feltham on 15th August 1963. There was an electric train service from Waterloo to Weybridge via Staines and Virginia Water, as well as the direct service to Woking. The main line is in the foreground. Trains from Waterloo thus arrived at Weybridge from both directions. Both lines are still open.

Plate 115: Class N, No. 31819 is turned on the turntable at Ascot on 19th May 1962, after working a freight from Feltham. There was a small engine shed here, long since demolished, which was situated at the other end of the station.

Plate 116: Class N, No. 31858 is pictured at Ascot on a wet morning in May 1962 with the daily freight from Woking via Frimley. On this occasion the train consisted of just one brake van. The platform seats in the foreground are of standard SR design and were to be found all over the system.

Plate 117 (above): Class M7, No. 30028 heads a railway enthusiasts' special and enters Frimley with two coach set No. 1 on 15th October 1960. The train started from Farnborough (main line) and after reversing at Frimley, proceeded to Bentley and Bordon and then on to Alton *(see Plate 124).*

WOKING TO WINCHESTER VIA ALTON

Although the main line from Woking to Winchester and Southampton ran via Basingstoke, there was a shorter route which left the main line at Pirbright Junction, west of Brookwood, and ran via Alton. The section from Pirbright to Farnham, which opened in 1865, gave the LSWR direct access to Aldershot in competition with the SER which was tapping the trade derived from military development in the area. The main line is, of course, still open, but the direct line now terminates at Alton, which was the limit of the pre-war electrification in this direction. Beyond Alton, the service was worked by steam and later by diesel multiple units until closure on 5th February 1973. The section between Ropley and Alresford is once again steam operated, now under the auspices of the Mid Hants Railway *(see map at Plate 41).*

Plate 118: There was a main postal sorting office at Woking which generated considerable traffic for the railway. Class M7, No. 30378, with a parcels train for Alton, prepares to leave Woking two days prior to Christmas 1961. Note the 'Danger overhead live wires' plate on the water tanks, hardly necessary within the third rail electrified area of the Western Section.

Plate 119: Class M7, No. 30378, one year later, on the same working just beyond Woking. In the background is the engineers' yard. The goods yard is opposite and runs alongside the junction with the Portsmouth line.

Plate 120: Another parcels train leaves Woking, with Class M7, No. 30055, at the end of 1962. For many years an M7 locomotive from Guildford shed was stationed at Woking for general shunting duties.

Plate 121: The Alton line left the main line on an embankment prior to entering a short tunnel on the edge of an army firing range. Class Q1, No. 33035 steams along this embankment between the junction and tunnel, with a Woking to Alton parcels train, on 20th December 1963. On occasions, when the main line was blocked due to engineering works or mishaps, Waterloo to Bournemouth trains were diverted via Alton, joining the main line again near Winchester.

Plate 122: Class U, No. 31800 is seen shunting at Aldershot on 9th June 1962 whilst en route for Alton.

Plate 123: Class 700, No. 30325 shunts wagons at Farnham. This engine spent several hours performing this duty, on 9th June 1962, then suddenly disappeared into the electric train depot. It reappeared about ten minutes later and charged through Farnham hauling a dead electric unit.

Plate 124: Class M7, No. 30028 waits at Alton with the 12.05 p.m. for Eastleigh on 8th October 1957. The following month, this service was taken over by diesel units. Alton was also the starting point for the steam hauled services to Fareham, via the Meon Valley, a route which closed in 1955, and to Basingstoke, this route closing in 1932. The Eastleigh trains connected with the electric services from Waterloo and a Waterloo train can be seen on the right of the picture.

Plate 125: Another study of Class 700, No. 30325, this time with an up freight from Eastleigh, at Medstead & Four Marks, on 18th April 1956.

PORTSMOUTH TO SALISBURY

There was a regular service between Portsmouth & Southsea and Salisbury. Trains were routed either via Eastleigh, which was the more direct route, or via Netley and Southampton. The lines diverged at Fareham and merged at Romsey. In the 14 miles between Fareham and Southampton there were nine intermediate stations, situated closer than any others on the SR outside the London suburban area. Through trains from the south coast to the Western Region added variety both in terms of motive power and rolling stock. Both routes are still open for passenger services, with the exception of the short stretch between Eastleigh and Romsey. All Salisbury trains have been diesel operated since September 1957.

Plate 126 (right): 'West Country' class, No. 34046 *Braunton* approaches Fareham with the 11.00 a.m. Plymouth Friary to Brighton, via Salisbury and Southampton, on 8th October 1957. This train also conveyed through coaches for Portsmouth & Southsea. The water crane on the platform ramp is of LSWR origin.

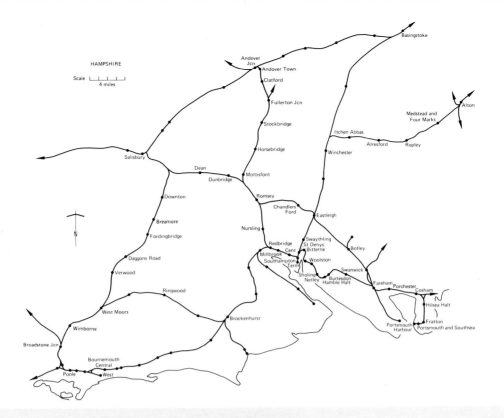

HAMPSHIRE

Scale |_|_|_|_|
4 miles

Basingstoke
Andover Jcn
Andover Town
Clatford
Fullerton Jcn
Stockbridge
Horsebridge
Alton
Medstead and Four Marks
Itchen Abbas
Alresford
Ropley
Winchester
Salisbury
Dean
Dunbridge
Mottisfont
Romsey
Chandlers Ford
Eastleigh
Downton
Nursling
Breamore
Fordingbridge
Redbridge
Cent
Millbrook
Southampton Term
Swaythling
St Denys
Bitterne
Botley
Daggons Road
Woolston
Verwood
Sholing
Netley
Swanwick
Burlesdon
Hamble Halt
Ringwood
Fareham
Porchester
Cosham
West Moors
Brockenhurst
Hilsea Halt
Wimborne
Portsmouth Harbour
Fratton
Portsmouth and Southsea
Broadstone Jcn
Bournemouth Central
Poole
West

Plate 127 (above left): A welcome return for a Class T9 a few years after regular steam trains ceased. No. 30117, with a special from Portsmouth Harbour to Eastleigh, via Southampton, is pictured at Fareham on 30th April 1961.

Plate 128 (above right): Class U, No. 31807, with the 9.00 a.m. Salisbury to Portsmouth & Southsea, approaches Southampton Central on 4th August 1957. The massive semaphore gantry in the background has now been replaced by colour light signals. This station was originally named Southampton West. After closure of Southampton Terminus, originally called the Town Station, the Central Station was renamed Southampton, the word 'Central' being dropped.

Plate 129: In more recent times, a double-headed special from Salisbury to Eastleigh, via Southampton, is hauled by Class 4MT, Nos. 80152 and 80016 and is seen near Nursling on 17th September 1966.

PORTSMOUTH TO ANDOVER

The service to Andover took the same routes to Romsey and left the Salisbury line at Kimbridge Junction. In addition to the local services, there were through trains to Cheltenham which used the ex-MSWJR from Andover via Swindon Town. Andover services were diesel operated from 4th November 1957.

Plate 130 (right upper): Railways in the Fareham area were further complicated by the provision of two lines in the Eastleigh direction. Just north of Fareham Station, there was a single track through a tunnel and double track to the west of the tunnel. These lines rejoined about two miles beyond Fareham, just before the junction for the Meon Valley line *(see Plate 124).* On 8th October 1957, Class M7, No. 30130, with set No. 328, approaches Fareham with the 2.45 p.m. from Andover Junction via Eastleigh.

Plate 131 (right lower): Class T9, No. 30726, heading Bulleid set No. 829, stops at Fareham with the 3.45 p.m. Portsmouth & Southsea to Andover Junction via Eastleigh train on 8th October 1957. The train in the other platform is the 11.00 a.m. from Plymouth.

Plate 132: The Andover train pictured at Eastleigh. Within a month this, and the remaining local services in the area, had become diesel unit operated. A fixed interval and more frequent service was introduced and passenger receipts increased dramatically in the first year of operation. On many occasions the two car units were overcrowded.

Plate 133: Class M7, No. 30480, with the 5.03 p.m. Romsey to Southampton Terminus, waits at Eastleigh on 5th August 1959. The train is composed of two loose coaches, an ex-LSWR brake third and a GWR brake third, and is probably a stand in for a failed diesel unit.

Plate 134: Class T9, No. 30287 and set No. 857 join the Waterloo to Bournemouth main line at Eastleigh with the 3.36 p.m. Andover Junction to Portsmouth & Southsea on 8th October 1957. After dieselization, the redundant T9s, which were used extensively on the Hampshire secondary lines, were stored at Eastleigh shed for many months prior to cutting up.

Plate 135: Class U, No. 31620 is pictured near Redbridge with a train of Western Region stock forming the 4.50 p.m. Southampton Terminus to Andover Junction train on 5th August 1959. The stretch of line from Southampton to Redbridge was a photographer's nightmare, with a background of factories, pylons, gasholders and other attributes of an industrial area.

Plate 136: Romsey is one of the few stations to remain virtually unchanged over the years. Even to the present day the main buildings are still intact and there is a small LSWR signal box at the junction of the Southampton and Eastleigh lines, just south of the station. Class T9, No. 30283, with the 1.53 p.m. Portsmouth & Southsea to Andover Junction via Eastleigh, makes a scheduled stop on 8th October 1957.

Plate 137: Class 700, No. 30309 is seen at Fullerton Junction with a special from Salisbury to Eastleigh, via Andover, on 2nd September 1962. This decrepit station, the second to be built at Fullerton, was in the 'V' of the junction with the Longparish branch which closed to passengers in 1931.

Plate 138: Another special heading for Andover, with Class Q, No. 30548, pictured near Mottisfont, in command on 18th April 1964. This line passed through some very pleasant countryside and followed the River Test for most of its length from the river-mouth at Redbridge.

Plate 139: The last day of passenger services between Andover and Romsey was 6th September 1964. Diesel unit No. 1130, with a Portsmouth bound train, leaves Mottisfont. The track and buildings were left intact for about three years after closure. In many ways, it would have been a suitable line for preservation, being on the edge of a holiday area. There were no substantial engineering works or weight restrictions and there was access to BR metals at each end. The facilities of Eastleigh Works were also not far away.

BOURNEMOUTH TO SALISBURY

The original main line from Southampton to Bournemouth ran via Ringwood and Wimborne. The SDJR from Bath joined this line at Wimborne where a reversal was necessary in order to reach Bournemouth. The junction was later resited at Broadstone obviating the need to reverse. The Bournemouth to Salisbury trains used the same route out of Bournemouth as far as West Moors, the first station beyond Wimborne. They then ran north-east towards Salisbury, joining the Romsey to Salisbury line at Alderbury Junction. The section between West Moors and Alderbury Junction was single track. Although a line of potential importance, offering a through route to the Midlands, it has always been overshadowed by the SDJR which was more convenient, scenically more interesting and offering a much greater variety of motive power.

Plate 140: Verwood, even in April 1964, had the air of the typical LSWR station, with a small signal box on the platform, the oil lamps, lower quadrant starter and, in the background, the public house.

Plate 141 (right upper): The 9.33 a.m. Salisbury to Bournemouth pictured at Verwood three weeks before closure on 4th May 1964. Class 4MT, No. 75003 and Bulleid set No. 793, are both rather more modern than the station.

Plate 142 (right lower): The same train on a previous occasion, 11th April 1964, drifting along near Three Legged Cross, which is situated between Verwood and West Moors. The engine is Class U, No. 31792 and the stock is a BR standard set.

Plate 143 (left upper):   Class N, No. 31814, with the Salisbury to Wimborne freight, shunts in the War Department Depot at West Moors on 30th August 1961.

Plate 144 (left lower):   West Moors was the junction for the Salisbury and Brockenhurst lines. Approaching, is the 12.50 p.m. Salisbury to Bournemouth West with Class 4MT, No. 76059 in charge. Waiting to leave, is Class U, No. 31637 with the 1.03 p.m. Bournemouth West to Salisbury train on 30th August 1961. The centre signal of the three on the gantry is for the War Department siding *(see Plate 143).*

Plate 145:   Class U, No. 31637 together with Bulleid set No. 854, form the Salisbury bound train. The vehicle in the bay is an S R bogie corridor parcels van, most of which by this time had been withdrawn from revenue earning service.

Plate 146:   Class S15, No. 30837 hauls the 5.05 p.m. Southampton Terminus to Wimborne, via Bournemouth Central, and is pictured at Broadstone on 30th August 1961. This was an exceptional routing in that most trains from Southampton or Brockenhurst for Wimborne, ran via Ringwood and terminated at Bournemouth West.

Plate 147: The 11.12 a.m. Wimborne t
Bournemouth West leaves Broadstone o
the dull morning of 18th April 1964. Th
engine is rebuilt 'West Country' class
No. 34028 *Eddystone*, with Bulleid se
No. 781.

Plate 148: Class 5MT, No. 73019 passe
Bournemouth West carriage sidings wit
the 12.43 p.m. from Poole on 10t
September 1959. The headcode is fo
the SDJR route, on which lamps, rathe
than discs, were used even in daytime.

Plate 149: Class U, No. 31633, with the 1.03 p.m. to Salisbury, climbs the 1 in 90 out of Bournemouth West on 10th September 1959. Bournemouth West lost more and more of its trains with the closure of the Salisbury line, the Ringwood loop and the SDJR, all within the space of two years. Bournemouth West Station closed in October 1965 and all trains now use Bournemouth Central.

WEST OF EXETER

The LSWR line from Exeter was opened as far as Okehampton in 1871. From there, a line was laid north-west toward Bude, although initially terminating at Holsworthy. The North Cornwall line proper began at Halwill, between Okehampton and Holsworthy, and was opened in sections over a period of thirteen years. The LSWR was anticipating that holiday traffic would be generated once Padstow was reached and that there would also be revenue from the transport of fish from Padstow and slate from Delabole quarries. The first train from Exeter to Padstow ran on 27th March 1899. There have always been through trains from London, the most famous being the 'Atlantic Coast Express'. Local services for North Cornwall and Bude started either at Okehampton or Exeter Central.

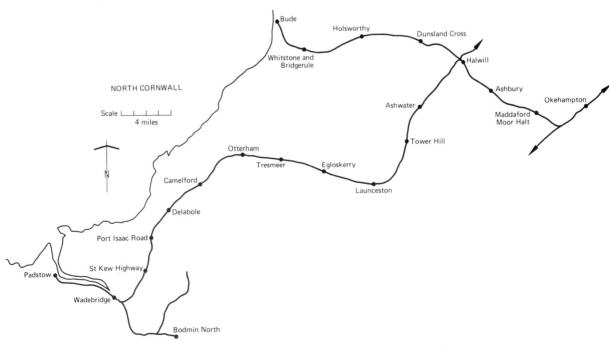

Plate 150: Class T9, No. 30729, with a loose Bulleid coach and two coach Maunsell set, pauses in the centre road at Exeter Central. It had just worked the 3.13 p.m. from Padstow on 11th August 1960.

Plate 151: Exeter St. David's and Exeter Central were at right angles to each other, at somewhat different elevations and separated by a tunnel. Most trains required banking up the 1 in 37 between the two stations. There was considerable freight traffic from North Cornwall and the heavier trains were also double-headed up the bank. Class Z, No. 30956 and an unidentified Class N locomotive emerge from the tunnel, lost in a cloud of smoke, on 12th August 1960.

Plate 152: For many years Class E1/R rebuilt Brighton tanks were used as bankers. These were replaced by Maunsell Class Z, 0-8-0 tank locomotives in 1960. Two Class Zs, Nos. 30955 and 30954 provide banking assistance at the rear of a ballast train from Meldon Quarry, which is situated just west of Okehampton.

Plate 153: Apart from the through portion of the 'Atlantic Coast Express', there were only four passenger trains on Monday to Friday over the North Cornwall line to Padstow. There was no Sunday service. Class T9, No. 30313 awaits departure from Okehampton with the 5.51 p.m. all stations to Padstow on 11th August 1960, a journey of 60 miles taking two hours.

Plate 154: Okehampton is on the northern edge of Dartmoor at an elevation of 700 ft. above sea level and, as a result, seems to suffer from more than its fair share of bad weather. The highest point on the Southern Railway was 950 ft. at Sourton, just beyond Meldon Junction. Class T9, No. 30717, in appalling condition, performs shunting duties at Okehampton in inclement weather on 11th August 1960.

Plate 155: Class T9, No. 30717 is fed and watered at Okehampton, prior to working the evening train to Launceston on 11th August 1960. The single road engine shed is seen in the background.

Plate 156: Class T9, No. 30313 shunts at Okehampton on the same day, during a brief respite from the drizzle drifting over the moor.

Plate 157: Meldon Quarry, the source of ballast for the whole of the Southern system. The coach on the left forms the quarryman's train, which had been worked from Okehampton on 11th August 1960 by the Class T9 locomotive, No. 30313, seen shunting. The coach is a BTK 'Matchboard', No. 3550, built for boat train use by the Metropolitan Carriage, Wagon & Finance Company to an SECR design.

Plate 158: A ballast train from Meldon, with the quarryman's coach, entering Okehampton and hauled by No. 30313 later on the same day.

HALWILL TO BUDE

Plate 159: Class N, No. 31837, with the 3.15 p.m. Bude to Okehampton, appoaches Halwill on 5th July 1961. The train consists of two Maunsell brake thirds and a four wheeled SR utility van. The North Cornwall line is seen diverging to the left.

Plate 160: The 'Atlantic Coast Express' had through coaches for virtually all West of England holiday resorts. At Halwill, the train split for Padstow and Bude. Class 3MT, No. 82018, with the Bude portion, consisting of set No. 178, prepares to leave Halwill on 10th April 1956.

Plate 161: Dunsland Cross was the first station on the Bude line west of Halwill and served several small communities, none of which was particularly near to the station. Class 3MT, No. 82017 is seen with the 1.45p.m. Bude to Okehampton train.

Plate 162: The next station towards Bude served Holsworthy, a market town of some importance. Class N, No. 31837 approaches Holsworthy with the 1.18 p.m. Okehampton to Bude on 5th July 1961. It can be seen that the station is electrically lit, as was Halwill, which was rather unusual for a country station.

Plate 163: The same train pictured at Holsworthy. BR standard cattle wagons served the local market, which still operates, once a week, many years after closure of the railway.

Plate 164: Class N, No. 31836 stands at Bude with the 7.02 p.m. to Halwill on 5th July 1961. The train comprises Maunsell set No. 198 and an ex-LMSR luggage brake van. There was a small engine shed at Bude to which was allocated one Mogul. There was also a short spur to Bude Wharf, but the whole area has now been redeveloped.

THE NORTH CORNWALL LINE

Plate 165: Class N, No. 31836 is pictured with the 12.58 p.m. (Saturdays only) Padstow to Exeter Central at Halwill on 5th July 1961. This train had through coaches to Waterloo. The through coaches from Bude can be seen being backed on to the rear of the train.

Plate 166: Class U1, No. 31904 leaves Halwill later in the day with the 3.13 p.m. Padstow to Exeter Central. The full name of the station is Halwill for Beaworthy, which can be seen on the large nameboard.

Plate 167: Halwill was one of those stations which saw great activity for short periods of the day, with trains arriving from all directions, combining or splitting as appropriate and departing, to leave an atmosphere of silence for hour upon hour. 'Battle of Britain' class, No. 34075 *264 Squadron* leaves Halwill with the 3.35 p.m. Okehampton to Wadebridge train on 5th July 1961. In the background is the Bude train.

Plate 168: Many of the trains were lightly loaded, even in the summer. 'West Country' class, No. 34011 *Tavistock* heads the Padstow portion of the 'Atlantic Coast Express', with a mere two coaches, on 5th July 1961. The location is Otterham, which was on the northern edge of Bodmin Moor.

Plate 169: Most of the intermediate stations on the North Cornwall line were in isolated locations, often a considerable distance from the place after which they were named. Camelford Station was almost two miles from the town and, according to the nameboard, optimistically served Boscastle and Tintagel. There were, in fact, connecting services operated by the Southern National Bus Company, although the time taken from arrival at Camelford, by train, to arrival at Boscastle, by bus, was about one hour, a distance by the most direct route of four miles. This view of Camelford Station was photographed on 2nd July 1961.

Plate 170: Class N, No. 31834 heads the 1.00 p.m. (Saturdays only) Padstow to Exeter Central, with through coaches to Waterloo, near Wadebridge on 1st July 1961. The short stretch of line from Wadebridge to the divergence of the North Cornwall and Bodmin routes was operated as two single lines.

Plate 171 (right upper): In the days before the Moguls arrived, most of the lighter trains were operated by Class T9 locomotives. Class T9, No. 30717 stands ready to leave Wadebridge on 2nd July 1958 with the 3.13 p.m. Padstow to Exeter Central train.

Plate 172 (right lower): Class N, No. 31834, with a freight train for Halwill, waits at Wadebridge on 1st July 1961. Beyond the coaling stage, on the right, was the motive power depot.

Plate 175: Padstow, a fishing port, a seaside resort and the most westerly outpost of the LSWR. In the carriage sidings, on 1st July 1961, is Class N, No. 31837 and on the quayside is an LSWR ironclad brake third in use by the engineers' department.

◁   *Plate 173 (left upper):*   Wadebridge was, for many years, the home of the three Beattie well tanks, retained for working the china clay trains from Wenfordbridge. They were also used as station pilots. Class 0298, No. 30586 backs on to set No. 70 on 1st July 1961. Note the brazier by the water column, a reminder that the West Country sometimes suffers severe winters.

◁   *Plate 174 (left lower):*   The down 'Atlantic Coast Express' on 3rd July 1961 crosses a tributary of the River Camel, six hours after leaving Waterloo which is 260 miles away. The engine in charge is the last member of the 'Battle of Britain' class, No. 34110 *66 Squadron.* The trackbed from Wadebridge to Padstow is now a public footpath.

Plate 176: Class T9, No. 30712 is pictured on the Padstow turntable on 2nd July 1958. This scene was repeated several times a day for so many years that no one looked twice, until one day it was no more.

Plate 177: The end of the day. Class T9, No. 30712 shunts stock at Padstow for the evening train to Wadebridge on 2nd July 1958.

Appendix One ~ Index of Locomotives

CLASS N1 (SECR)	*Plate No.*
No. 31878	91

CLASS N15 (SR)

No. 30799	7

CLASS Q (SR)

No. 30537	68, 69
No. 30545	110
No. 30548	138

CLASS Q1 (SR)

No. 33010	112
No. 33018	42
No. 33033	25
No. 33035	46, 55, 120
No. 33038	26

CLASS R1 (SER)

No. 31107	9

CLASS S15 (SR)

No. 30833	114
No. 30835	Front, 31
No. 30837	113, 146
No. 30839	109

CLASS T9 (LSWR)

No. 30117	127
No. 30120	85
No. 30283	136
No. 30287	134
No. 30313	153, 156–8
No. 30712	176, 177
No. 30717	154, 155, 171
No. 30718	107
No. 30726	131, 132
No. 30729	150

CLASS U (SR)

No. 31620	135
No. 31625	49
No. 31631	50
No. 31633	149
No. 31637	144, 145
No. 31638	32, 37
No. 31639	38
No. 31791	44
No. 31792	142
No. 31800	122
No. 31807	128

CLASS U1 (SR)

No. 31892	68, 99
No. 31898	59
No. 31899	60
No. 31904	95, 166

CLASS V (SR)

No. 30924	12
No. 30938	28
No. 30939	11

'WEST COUNTRY CLASS' (SR/BR)

No. 34009	62
No. 34011	168
No. 34021	13
No. 34028	147
No. 34046	126

'BATTLE OF BRITAIN' CLASS (SR/BR)

No. 34055	93
No. 34067	9
No. 34068	106
No. 34075	167
No. 34077	21
No. 34085	3
No. 34086	111
No. 34110	174

CLASS Z (SR)	*Plate No.*
No. 30954	152
No. 30955	152
No. 30956	151

CLASS O298 (LSWR)

No. 30586	173

CLASS 700 (LSWR)

No. 30309	137
No. 30325	123, 125

CLASS 4300 (GWR)

No. 5385	41

CLASS 7800 (GWR)

No. 7808	35

CLASS 4MT (LMSR)

No. 42076	10
No. 42077	6
No. 42095	5, 19
No. 42106	75

CLASS 2MT (BR)

No. 84021	17
No. 84029	20

CLASS 3MT (BR)

No. 82017	161
No. 82018	160
No. 82029	20

CLASS 4MT (BR) 2-6-4T

No. 80012	76
No. 80013	83
No. 80016	86, 129
No. 80018	30
No. 80034	24
No. 80037	82, 83
No. 80040	16, 57
No. 80054	81
No. 80067	96
No. 80082	77
No. 80085	22, 23
No. 80095	45, 74
No. 80138	51
No. 80142	56, 73
No. 80143	29
No. 80144	78
No. 80149	88
No. 80150	103, 104
No. 80151	43
No. 80152	129
No. 80154	80

CLASS 4MT (BR) 4-6-0

No. 75003	141
No. 75069	58
No. 75075	64

CLASS 4MT (BR) 2-6-0

No. 76031	53
No. 76059	144

CLASS 5MT (BR)

No. 73019	148
No. 73086	1

DIESEL ELECTRIC 'HAMPSHIRE' UNIT

No. 1130	139

Appendix Two ~ Index of Rolling Stock

Set No.	Composition			Origin	Plate No.
1	6488 BCL	1066 T		LSWR/SECR push-pull	117
24	2832 BTK	6602 BCK		Maunsell	153
70	4378 BTK	6707 BCK		Bulleid	173
83	4017 BTK	29 TK	5826 CK	Bulleid	57
	4018 BTK				
85	4022 BTK	31 TK	5828 CK	Bulleid	41
	4021 BTK				
90	4031 BTK	36 TK	5833 CK	Bulleid	82
	4032 BTK				
91	4033 BTK	37 TK	5834 CK	Bulleid	15
	4034 BTK				
92	4035 BTK	5835 CK	4036 BTK	Bulleid	52
94	4039 BTK	40 TK	5837 CK	Bulleid	20
	4040 BTK				
178	2836 BTK	6690 BCK		Maunsell	160
181	4087 BTK	5173 CK	5174 CK	Maunsell	60, 99
	4088 BTK				
182	3715 BTK	5613 CK	5614 CK	Maunsell	89
	4090 BTK				
186	3694 BTK	5604 CK	5605 CK	Maunsell	27
	3695 BTK				
187	3696 BTK	5606 CK	5607 CK	Maunsell	50, 92
	3697 BTK				
188	3698 BTK	5608 CK	5609 CK	Maunsell	59, 97
	3699 BTK				
189	3704 BTK	5618 CK	5619 CK	Maunsell	98
	3705 BTK				
191	3708 BTK	5622 CK	5623 CK	Maunsell	95
	3709 BTK				
194	3740 BTK	5642 CK	3741 BTK	Maunsell	74
198	2780 BTK	6699 BCK		Maunsell	164
227	2755 BTK	5670 CK	2758 BTK	Maunsell	96
248	2779 BTK	54 TK	2781 BTK	Maunsell/Bulleid	90
328	3797 BTK	5638 CK	3798 BTK	Maunsell	130
444	3695 BTK	5605 CK		Maunsell	45
451	4071 BTK	5164 CK	5163 CK	Maunsell	91
	4072 BTK				
456	3711 BTK	5629 CK		Maunsell	43
460	3677 BTK	978 TK	5507 CK	Maunsell (8 set)	9
	5505 CK	5506 CK	5508 CK		
	979 TK	3562 BTK			
460	4068 BTK	5160 CK		Maunsell (2 set)	54
504	3820 BTK	6236 CK		LBSCR push-pull	4, 101
608	6689 BCK	1330 TO		Maunsell push-pull	86
609	6694 BCK	1353 TO		Maunsell push-pull	87
610	6679 BCK	1317 TO		Maunsell push-pull	46
651	6941 BC			LBSCR push-pull	4
652	6428 BC	1074 T		LSWR push-pull	63, 65, 67, 71
656	3542 BT	5499 C		SECR push-pull	70
659	6409 BC	3324 BT		SECR push-pull	91
660	3505 BT	5473 C		SECR push-pull	61
715	3847 BT			LBSCR push-pull	102–104
770	4301 BTK	1496 TO	1501 TO	Bulleid	110
	1491 TO	1463 TO	1503 TO		
	1486 TO	1452 TO	1465 TO		
	4302 BTK				
781	4323 BTK	5762 CK	4324 BTK	Bulleid	147
793	4347 BTK	5774 CK	4348 BTK	Bulleid	141
829	4297 BTK	5822 CK	4298 BTK	Bulleid	131, 132
854	2509 BTK	5912 CK	2510 BTK	Bulleid	145
857	2515 BTK	5915 CK	2516 BTK	Bulleid	134
953	4233 BTK	5693 CK	4234 BTK	Maunsell	81
955	4237 BTK	5695 CK	4238 BTK	Maunsell	22, 23
964	2843 BTK	5710 CK	2844 BTK	Bulleid	5
972	2859 BTK	5718 CK	2860 BTK	Bulleid	11
974	2863 BTK	5720 CK	2864 BTK	Bulleid	35
977	2869 BTK	5723 CK	2870 BTK	Bulleid	47, 48